Reinventing the Command Pattern

The Art of Undoable Operations

Table of Contents

Chapter 1. Introduction

In this Special Report, we delve into the intricate realm of the "Command Pattern" - an essential chapter in the comprehensive annals of software design patterns. The feature titled "Reinventing the Command Pattern: The Art of Undoable Operations" rethinks traditional concepts, inspiring software engineers to construct robust applications with unprecedented efficiency. With the aid of real-world examples, we meticulously dissect the nuts and bolts of undoable operations, striving to make this advanced concept accessible and engaging even for the uninitiated. This pragmatic exploration into one of the most potent software engineering techniques promises to be a valuable resource, whether you're an experienced developer wanting to refine your craft, or a newcomer eager to get a solid understanding of software design principles.

Chapter 2. Demystifying the Command Pattern

Undoing an operation usually proves to be as crucial as executing it, especially when working with applications that involve a host of transactions. In this context, the Command Pattern offers our applications a powerful advantage, by allowing us to encapsulate an operation (including its parameters) within an object. The programming paradigm could then execute the encapsulated operation using `execute()`, or cancel the effects with `unexecute()`, resulting in undoable operations.

2.1. The Command Pattern Unveiled

In essence, the Command Pattern is a behavioral design pattern that encapsulates a request as an object, thereby allowing clients to parameterize operations with different requests, queue, or even log requests, and support undoable operations. How is this accomplished? It's all about transforming a request into a standalone object which contains all the information about the request. This transformation lets you pass the request as a method parameter, delay it, store the history of requests, and even manipulate requests.

Here's a barebones example of implementing the Command pattern in Java:

```java
interface Command {
    void execute();
}

class LightOnCommand implements Command {
    private Light light;
```

```
    public LightOnCommand(Light light) {
        this.light = light;
    }

    public void execute() {
        light.switchOn();
    }
}
```

The Command interface here has a method execute(), which is the function held responsible for executing the operation. The LightOnCommand class encapsulates a request to turn on the light.

Chapter 3. Backing the Command Pattern with Real-World Examples

One doesn't have to look too far for real-world examples of the Command Pattern. Think of a smart home equipped with a universal remote control which can command lights, the air conditioner, or the television with the press of a button.

Let's consider the `execute()` method for the framework of this universal controller. Each device – the light, the TV, and the AC – will have a different implementation of the `execute()` method defined. For instance, if you press the button corresponding to the light, it executes the `lightOn()` method. In a similar fashion, for the TV, it runs the `turnOnTV()` function, and for the AC, it triggers the `acOn()` method.

```
class UniversalRemote {
    private Command command;

    void setCommand(Command command){
        this.command = command;
    }

    void pressButton(){
        command.execute();
    }
}
```

Now, the `UniversalRemote` class does not need to know what device this is or what `execute()` does for this device. All it needs to know is that it needs to call the `execute()` method when the button is pressed.

Chapter 4. The Command Pattern Approached Differently: Undoing Actions

The domain of the command pattern is not confined to the execution of an operation, but it can also span undoing the operation. Sandwiched between these two operations - the executing and undoing - lies a sphere of many transactions happening concurrently, where being able to undo some of them might be necessary.

Typically, a command object consists of the execute() method that executes the operation and an unexecute() method that undoes the previously performed operation. Every execute() operation should keep track of its history to aid the unexecute() operation. Here's a typical example of how to implement this:

```
interface Command {
    void execute();
    void unexecute();
}

class LightOnCommand implements Command {
    private Light light;

    public LightOnCommand(Light light) {
        this.light = light;
    }

    public void execute() {
        light.switchOn();
    }

    public void unexecute() {
```

```
        light.switchOff();
    }
}
```

The controller framework would then look like this:

```
class UniversalRemote {
    private Command command;

    void setCommand(Command command){
        this.command = command;
    }

    void pressButton(){
        command.execute();
    }

    void pressUndo(){
        command.unexecute();
    }
}
```

Chapter 5. Implementing a Command History

A command history is how we can keep track of requests. With a history stack in place, we are not just enabling the undo of the most recent command, but we can provide the ability to undo a series of commands. For this, we need a history stack to keep track of commands executed and in what order. This will look like the following:

```java
class RemoteControlWithUndo {
    private Stack<Command> history = new Stack<>();

    void setCommand(Command command){
        this.command = command;
    }

    void pressButton(){
        command.execute();
        history.push(command);
    }

    void pressUndo(){
        if(!history.isEmpty()){
            Command command = history.pop();
            command.unexecute();
        }
    }
}
```

Here, the `history` stack keeps track of all the commands. When you press the Undo button, it will execute `unexecute()` on the most recent command.

Chapter 6. Wrapping Up

The Command Pattern allows us to encapsulate a request as an object, thereby decoupling the sender of the request from its receiver. This segregation allows us to parameterize different requests, queue requests, offer a history log, and manage undo operations. It's a versatile pattern — one that, when implemented correctly, can add a massive degree of flexibility and control to applications.

Chapter 7. Undoable Operations: The Hidden Art

The Command Pattern, a cornerstone of behavioral patterns, sets forth an important principle for software design - encapsulate a request as an object, allowing the manipulation of requests such as parameterization, queuing, and more critically, undoing operations. This element of the Command Pattern distinguishes itself as the focal point of our exploration. By shaping our understanding of undoable operations, we blaze a trail towards versatile and resilient software design.

7.1. The Anatomy of Undoable Operations

Undoable operations, in simple terms, allow users to revert an action and return the system back to its previous state. This characteristic bestows a sense of freedom upon users, offering them room for experiments and mistakes. Here is the broad anatomy of a typical undoable operation.

1. The Command Interface

```
public interface Command {
    void execute();
    void undo();
}
```

Commands maintain a binding between a receiver object and an action. Implementations of the Command interface must provide the execute() method that carries out the operation, and an undo() method that reverts such an operation.

1. Concrete Command Class

```java
public class ConcreteCommand implements Command {
  private Receiver receiver;
  private State preExecutionState;

  public ConcreteCommand(Receiver receiver) {
    this.receiver = receiver;
  }

  public void execute() {
    preExecutionState = receiver.getState();
    receiver.action();
  }

  public void undo() {
    receiver.setState(preExecutionState);
  }
}
```

Maintaining the preExecutionState in the ConcreteCommand allows us to revert to the previous state when undo() is invoked. Here, the undo() method does not repeat the execute() method in reverse, but instead, it restores the previous state.

1. Invoker

```java
public class Invoker {
  private Command command;

  public Invoker(Command command) {
    this.command = command;
  }

  public void runCommand() {
```

```java
        command.execute();
    }

    public void rollBackStackedCommands(){
        command.undo();
    }
}
```

The `Invoker` is our user-facing entity, which triggers command execution and undoing actions. As such, it maintains a history stack of all executed commands to facilitate multiple command undoing.

7.2. Incorporating the Undo into the Pattern

Integrating the undo operation into the command pattern results in a robust structure. Implementing an undo operation can be as simple as storing the previous state before the execution of an operation. However, it's critical to ascertain that the state stays consistent following undo operations in multithreaded environments.

7.3. The Curse of Complexity: Multilevel Undo

When we allow multiple undo operations, we introduce a new level of complexity to our design, referred to as Multilevel Undos. To apply this feature, we need to keep track of a list of past states or past commands in LIFO order. When an undo operation is issued, the action associated with the most recent command is undone, and that command is popped from the command history.

```java
public class Invoker {
```

```java
    private Stack<Command> commandStack;

    public Invoker() {
        this.commandStack = new Stack<>();
    }

    public void runCommand(Command command) {
        command.execute();
        commandStack.push(command);
    }

    public void rollBackStackedCommands() {
        if (!commandStack.isEmpty()) {
            commandStack.pop().undo();
        }
    }
}
```

Here, the `Invoker` maintains a `Stack` of `Command` objects. When `runCommand()` is invoked, the `Command` object is added to the stack, and `rollBackStackedCommands()` pops a `Command` from the stack and calls its `undo()` method.

7.4. The Resource Intensive Nature of Undo Operations

While helpful, undoing operations and state preservation can be resource-intensive, especially in scenarios dealing with large datasets or longer operation history. It's crucial to understand the trade-off and weigh benefits against the cost of additional resources.

7.5. Summary

Undoable operations render our software applications robust and user-friendly. By capturing previous states or actions, we can implement undo features, allowing us to revert our systems to prior states. Notwithstanding the resource demand and complexity, the application of undoable operations via the Command Pattern can significantly improve your software design. The command pattern encapsulates an operation as an object, abstracts the performer from the action, and accommodates additional features like undoing actions, queuing commands, or even extending the base commands. It is a valuable resource for software developers, providing tools to design advanced, high-utility software applications.

Chapter 8. Context and Foundations of the Command Pattern

The origins of the Command Pattern trace back to the advent of computer software. The structured and strategic programming concepts that evolved demanded an organized way to deal with functions, actions, or operations, which eventually gave birth to this design pattern. The Command Pattern not only aids in effectively structuring systems but also enhances their adaptability and testability.

=== Command Pattern's Cornerstone: Encapsulation

Command Pattern's foundational concept is Encapsulation—the idea of bundling data and methods that manipulate that data within an object to guard it from external interference and misuse. Encapsulation provisions software development with the ability to hide or reveal complexities and intricacies of an operation.

Consider an archetypal example of a remote-controlled device, where each button renders a specific functionality—turning the device on/off, adjusting volume, or changing channels. Here, end users interact with these simple, encapsulated operations without being concerned with their underlying complexity. In essence, with the Command Pattern, we encapsulate these requests (i.e., operations) into separate command objects with a common interface.

Each command in the Command pattern is typically characterized by an interface with an 'execute' method. This command instance incapsulates the action to be taken and its parameters.

```
public interface Command {
```

```
    void execute();
}
```

Next, let's implement this interface in a concrete command class:

```
public class LightOnCommand implements Command {
    Light light; //receiver

    public LightOnCommand(Light light) {
        this.light = light; //has a reference to the
receiver object
    }


    public void execute() {
        light.on(); }
}
```

As illustrated above, the receiver object (Light) and the operation
(on) are encapsulated in the command object (LightOnCommand) via
encapsulation.

=== Decoupling in Command Pattern

The Command Pattern promotes "decoupling"—a practice to make
software components independent and, hence, interchangeable by
minimizing direct dependencies among components. The Command
Pattern ensures decoupling between the sender (button press or
invoker) and the receiver (device functionality or operand).

The diagram below illustrates traditionally 'coupled' sender and
receiver, before decoupling. This sort of close coupling is susceptible
to changes and often leads to significant efforts to accommodate
minor changes.

```
actor Sender
actor Receiver
Sender -- Receiver : "Standard Procedure"
```

However, after implementing the Command pattern, the sender only knows about a command that it can invoke, and the receiver is wholly encapsulated within the command. Thus, various receivers can execute different commands without the sender knowing the details.

```
actor Sender
object "Concrete\nCommand 1" as Command1
object "Concrete\nCommand 2" as Command2
actor Receiver
Sender -- Command1 : "execute() (Command1)"
Command1 -- Receiver : "action() (Command1)"
Sender -- Command2 : "execute() (Command2)"
Command2 -- Receiver : "action() (Command2)"
```

Without the Command Pattern, we would need multiple conditional statements to cover all possible actions, leading to complex and inferior code. As the demand grows, this code would be hard to maintain and prone to errors. The enhanced decoupling implemented via Command pattern helps in eliminating this repercussion and provides a more elegant and efficient code structure.

=== Undo and Redo Operations

Frequent users of various software applications would be no stranger to undo (Ctrl + Z) and redo (Ctrl + Y) functionalities. Developers deliver this functionality using the Command Pattern. The idea is to create an additional 'undo' method that performs the inverse of the 'execute' method, effectively canceling its effects.

Here's a glimpse of how this can look in the code:

```java
public interface Command {
  void execute();
  void undo();
}
```

An implementation can look like:

```java
public class LightOnCommand implements Command {
    Light light;
    public LightOnCommand(Light light) {
        this.light = light;
    }

    public void execute() {
        light.on();
    }

    public void undo() {
        light.off();
    }
}
```

The Command Pattern enables this undo ability by maintaining a history of executed Command objects. When requested, they can logically reverse an operation through the 'undo' method.

In conclusion, the Command Pattern's success lies in its simplicity and enhanced decoupling. By understanding encapsulation and the power of abstract command objects, developers are prepared to write more robust, maintainable, and efficient code. We've covered the historical context, foundations, and basic functionalities of the Command Pattern, giving you the groundwork to explore this powerful tool further. The next part of the report will further dissect this pattern, helping you find ways to enhance and diversify the Command Pattern's use in your software development endeavours.

Chapter 9. Principles of Reversibility

The idea of reversibility essentially refers to the concept of rolling back or "undoing" a specific series of tasks or operations, reverting the current system state to a previous one. It's a vital function in a wide array of applications, ranging from text editors to graphic design software, and even extending to complex ERP systems.

Let's dive in step by step to unravel the concepts and principles behind reversibility.

9.1. Understanding The Need for Reversibility

Imagine yourself working on a complex graphics design application for hours. You apply multiple effects, make color adjustments, and add various graphic elements. Suddenly, you realize that the last few adjustments don't look as promising as you've expected. At this point, the "undo" function becomes your savior, allowing you to revert those changes without affecting your prior work.

This is a practical example where reversibility proves itself to be a blessing. Without it, users would have to either manually reverse their actions, which would be tedious and cumbersome, or live with their errors.

9.2. Trailblazing with Command Pattern

Designing an application or system to be reversibly is not inherently straightforward. Here, the Command Pattern shines as a classic design pattern developed to handle these sorts of scenarios.

The command pattern encapsulates a request as an object, thereby letting developers parameterize clients with different requests, queues, or requests, and support undoable operations. This inherent quality of the Command Pattern makes it apt for handling the reversibility principle in software design.

9.3. An Insight into Command and its Receiver

A command in the Command Pattern is an object of a class that contains a method, symbolizing the operation to be performed, and a receiver, which understands the intricacies of how to perform the operation.

The central working principle of the Command Pattern revolves around these command objects, which are treated in the system as first-class citizens that can be created, manipulated, and extended to support new commands.

9.4. Figuring Out the Receiver

The receiver is an object that knows how to perform a set of actions. It's the workhorse of the Command Pattern. While the command designates "what" should be done, the receiver embodies "how" the task must be executed. By segregating these two aspects, we establish an environment conducive to reversibility.

9.5. Simple Undo Operations

While we can significantly leverage the command pattern, certain scenarios require something less complex than maintaining the list of all actions performed. A simple action that needs to be undone, akin to toggling a light switch on and off, does not necessitate the overhead of a full-blown command pattern principle.

In such a scenario, we introduce the concept of a dual command, where every operation has an equivalent opposing operation, making reversing an operation as simple as performing the opposing operation.

9.6. Implementing Complex Undoable Operations

In real life, operations are not always as straightforward as toggling a light switch. Applications often necessitate multiple interrelated actions, each of which must be carefully handled to ensure proper functioning.

In such cases, an operation cannot merely be reversed by executing a reversed order of instructions. Instead, we require a thorough and systematic way to capture the application's state before the operation and then reverse it to that specific state when an undo operation is requested.

9.7. Making Use of Mementos

To store the state of an application, we introduce the Memento pattern. This design pattern provides a capability to restore an object to its previous state using a so-called "memento" object.

The application can request a memento of the state before performing an operation from the receiver. If an undo operation is required, the application uses the memento to restore the object to its prior state effectively.

These mementos, however, must be handled carefully. Their misuse could lead to a discrepancy between the actual system state and the perceived state presented through the sequence of undo and redo operations.

9.8. Seeing the Bigger Picture

Undeniably, the principles of reversibility concern more than just individual operations. It's essential to consider the system's overall state and orchestrate the undoable operations, ensuring that they don't interfere with each other.

It's crucial to understand how the general state of the application should be stored, how undo stacks should be maintained efficiently, and how to handle potential conflicts between various instances of mementos.

9.9. Wrapping it Up

Comprehending and applying the principles of reversibility might appear daunting. However, when managed effectively, it provides a significant enhancement to user experience, and saves developers from innumerable potential inconsistencies and errors.

Design patterns such as the Command or Memento patterns, along with a well-architected undo and redo system, can pave the way for clean interfaces, easy error correction, and an overall seamless user experience.

Remember, software design is as much a creative art as it is a science, and the principles of reversibility affirm this statement. It's up to you, the developer, to sculpt these principles into your unique masterpiece of software.

In the next section, we will see these principles in action, scrutinizing real-world examples showing how various software implements reversibility and how these guiding principles can be leveraged for application development.

Chapter 10. Command Pattern: Classic Implementation

The essence of the Command Pattern is to encapsulate a request as an object, thereby letting you parameterize other objects with queues, requests, and operations. The encapsulated commands can even be executed at different times and can support undoable actions. To appreciate the beauty of this design pattern, let's start with a classic implementation.

We will begin with a naive approach and later refine it, employing the Command Pattern. In our scenario, we have an application that remotely manages a home automation system, controlling devices like lights, television, and air conditioning.

10.1. The Naive Approach

In a typical object-oriented programming fashion, we could have an interface called `Device`, and classes like `Light`, `Television`, and `AirConditioning` implementing it. Each of these classes will have methods such as `turnOn()` and `turnOff()`.

Our `RemoteControl` class should be flexible enough to control any device. For now, let's assume it only has two buttons: on and off. Here's a rudimentary implementation:

```
public interface Device {
    void turnOn();
    void turnOff();
}
```

```java
public class Light implements Device {
    @Override
    public void turnOn() {
        System.out.println("Turning on the light");
    }

    @Override
    public void turnOff() {
        System.out.println("Turning off the light");
    }
}

public class RemoteControl {
    private Device device;

    public RemoteControl(Device device) {
        this.device = device;
    }

    public void pressOn() {
        device.turnOn();
    }

    public void pressOff() {
        device.turnOff();
    }
}
```

Though the above code gives us flexibility in swapping devices using the `RemoteControl` class, if we want to extend the capabilities of the `RemoteControl` with an undo operation, we will run into issues.

10.2. Introducing the Command Pattern

The Command Pattern allows us to encapsulate each request into a separate object. We introduce a `Command` interface with methods `execute()` and `undo()`. Each device-specific command will implement this interface.

```java
public interface Command {
    void execute();
    void undo();
}

public class LightOnCommand implements Command {
    private Light light;

    public LightOnCommand(Light light) {
        this.light = light;
    }

    @Override
    public void execute() {
        light.turnOn();
    }

    @Override
    public void undo() {
        light.turnOff();
    }
}

public class LightOffCommand implements Command {
    private Light light;

    public LightOffCommand(Light light) {
```

```java
        this.light = light;
    }

    @Override
    public void execute() {
        light.turnOff();
    }

    @Override
    public void undo() {
        light.turnOn();
    }
}
```

Now, let's revise the RemoteControl class to use these Commands.

```java
public class RemoteControl {
    private Command onCommand;
    private Command offCommand;

    public RemoteControl(Command onCommand, Command
offCommand){
        this.onCommand = onCommand;
        this.offCommand = offCommand;
    }

    public void pressOn() {
        onCommand.execute();
    }

    public void pressOff() {
        offCommand.execute();
    }

    public void pressUndo() {
```

```
        onCommand.undo();
        offCommand.undo();
    }
}
```

Notice how our client code now couples to the Command interface rather than to concrete device objects. However, this quick hack does not yet implement the undo operation correctly.

10.3. Implementing Undo Correctly

The undo operation should undo the last executed command. So, we should store the last executed command and call undo() on it when needed. Let's update our RemoteControl class accordingly.

```
public class RemoteControl {
    private Command onCommand;
    private Command offCommand;
    private Command lastCommand;

    // constructor and pressOn, pressOff methods remain
the same...

    public void pressUndo() {
        lastCommand.undo();
    }
}
```

Now any time we call execute() on a command, we must update the lastCommand field. Hence, the pressOn() and pressOff() now look like this:

```
public void pressOn() {
```

```java
    onCommand.execute();
    lastCommand = onCommand;
}

public void pressOff() {
    offCommand.execute();
    lastCommand = offCommand;
}
```

There we have it: encapsulation of commands as objects, which now allows us easy execution of undo operations.

Understanding and mastering the Command Pattern is an important skill in software engineering, allowing you to write more flexible and extensible code which can support operations like undo and redo, queueing requests or even executing them at different times. This classic structural design pattern will indeed be an indispensable addition to your tool kit.

Chapter 11. Command Pattern: Challenges

Let's start our detailed excursion into the challenges associated with the Command Pattern in software design. Even though this pattern significantly improves the design and structure of software systems, it introduces its own set of complexity barriers, which we shall address methodically.

11.1. Understanding the Problem Space

The initial challenge lies in grasping the problem space for which the Command Pattern is optimal. It can be overly complicated or unnecessary to use this pattern for simple, modest systems. Understanding when to implement it is pivotal, as its improper usage can result in excessive abstraction layers, leading to difficult comprehension and maintenance.

11.2. Code Complexity

The Command Pattern often leads to an increase in code complexity. Each command in the pattern is a class itself, which might get overwhelming when handling a multitude of commands. This complexity aggravates as the addition of undo and redo operations demands each command class to include methods for executing and reverting the operation. Also, commands' dependency on receivers to capture their actions can lead to a profusion of code spread across numerous files.

11.3. Chaining Commands

Let's now turn our attention to chaining commands, which, while providing greater flexibility, also results in a compounded complexity. Picturing the operation flow in a command chain sometimes becomes challenging due to the large number of command objects. Additionally, the necessity for commands to communicate can introduce adherence problems to the Single Responsibility Principle (SRP).

11.4. Managing State

State management is another momentous challenge. Allowing commands to undo their effects requires them to keep track of the system state before their execution. When dealing with large objects, this could lead to substantial memory usage. On top of that, in multithreaded scenarios, ensuring state consistency between concurrent commands introduces additional complication.

11.5. Testing

In the testing realm, the Command Pattern often requires you to set up complex environments to ensure nominal operation. Specifically, the capacity to verify that commands properly maintain their state, notably in failure scenarios, becomes a challenging endeavour. This places a non-trivial burden on the development team to establish a comprehensive suite of tests covering all possible command interactions.

11.6. Serializing Commands

The process of serializing commands for storage or network transmission presents its own hurdles. Commands encapsulate not only operations but also state, particularly for undoable commands.

Therefore, serializing and deserializing commands needs careful planning to ensure state preservation, resulting in a more intricate serialization process compared to primitive data types.

11.7. Scalability and Performance

Last, but certainly not least, the Command Pattern may pressure performance in memory-constrained systems. Each command represents an object stored in memory, and in high-performance environments, the creation, and deletion of these objects can be costly. Additional considerations such as the time complexity involved in command execution and undo operations can also impact the system's performance.

In the following sections, we will introduce strategies to mitigate these challenges. However, it's clear that the Command Pattern, for all its significant advantages, has to be applied judiciously. Knowing these potential pitfalls is the first step toward constructing robust and adaptable software systems.

Chapter 12. Under the Hood: Redefining Undoable Operations

Undoable operations can play a vital role in creating robust and user-friendly software applications. Particularly in domains prone to user errors, having the facility to revert or undo actions is a feature that could exceedingly elevate the user experience.

The conventional approach in implementing undoable operations leverages the Command Pattern — a behavioral design pattern that turns a request into a standalone object, containing all the information necessary to execute the request.

12.1. The Classic Command Pattern

Let's start by providing an overview of the classic Command pattern. At its core, the Command pattern involves encapsulating each action or operation as an object. This encapsulation allows for parameterization of commands, requests, or operations. These objects can be stored, passed around, and invoked as per the requirement.

The participants in the classic Command Pattern include:

- The Command: Defines an interface for executing an operation.

- ConcreteCommand: Extends the command and binds it with a receiver to execute the corresponding action.

- Client: Creates a ConcreteCommand object and sets its receiver.

- Invoker: Asks the command to execute the request.

- Receiver: Knows how to perform the operations associated with carrying out a request.

A simple Java example to illustrate a classic Command pattern is a Light Switch application, where 'turning on' and 'turning off' the light are the operations:

`` public interface Command { void execute(); }

public class LightOnCommand implements Command { private Light light; public LightOnCommand(Light light) { this.light = light; } public void execute() { light.turnOn(); } }

public class LightOffCommand implements Command { private Light light; public LightOffCommand(Light light) { this.light = light; } public void execute() { light.turnOff(); } } `` Here, LightOnCommand and LightOffCommand are the ConcreteCommands which possess the action to be performed by them.

12.2. Extending Command Pattern for Undoable Operations

A primary way to empower the command pattern to support undoable operations involves extending the Command interface to include an additional method, namely 'undo'.

```
public interface Command {
    void execute();
    void undo();
}
```

Each ConcreteCommand then needs to implement this undo method with behavior that reverses the outcome of the corresponding execute method.

In our Light example, the undo action for a "light on" operation would be to "turn off the light", and vice versa:

```java
public class LightOnCommand implements Command {
    ...
    public void undo() {
        light.turnOff();
    }
}

public class LightOffCommand implements Command {
    ...
    public void undo() {
        light.turnOn();
    }
}
```

In order to perform an undo operation, we would need to keep track of the operations that have happened. The most naive approach could be using a stack to store the commands.

This adjustment to the Undoable Command pattern allows for a more dynamic and interactive user experience. Software developers can now have each action or operation immediately prepared to be undone, providing a 'safety net' for users.

12.3. Conclusion

The Command Pattern, with its extension for undoable operations, provides a robust and flexible structure for dynamic application behavior. It simplifies the relation between objects and enables a broad spectrum of functionality, including queuing of commands, tracking their history, and enabling undo and redo functionalities.

Through real-world examples, we have deconstructed the

fundamental concepts of Redefining Undoable Operations. Remember, these patterns are mere tools at your disposal - their true effectiveness lies in the hands of the craftsman deploying them. It is recommended that the approach chosen always caters to the complexity of the operations and the coherence with the larger application architecture.

This comprehensive exploration of one of the most potent software engineering techniques will be a valuable resource for refining your craft. It paves the path for not just understanding the concept but mastering it, ready to take on enhanced software application development with newfound confidence and proficiency.

Chapter 13. Case Studies: Success Stories of Undoable Operations

In our investigation of the Command Pattern, the case studies provide invaluable context, showcasing its real-world applications. Through analyses of these success stories, this content aims to elucidate the art of crafting undoable operations, underscoring the potential of the Command Pattern to streamline complex software systems.

13.1. The Retentive Text Editor

A text editor represents an ideal stage for the Command Pattern. In particular, the 'undo' functionality epitomizes an undoable operation. The command to add, remove, or modify text maps concisely onto the pattern and then enables the undo operation.

Considering the Command Pattern

```cpp
class Command {
public:
    virtual ~Command() {}
    virtual void execute() = 0;
    virtual void undo() = 0;
};
```

Each command issued (add, delete, modify) implements this interface, storing the state before it gets executed. Undoing the command is as simple as restoring the state from before the execution.

To manage commands, we utilize a command manager, itself a careful implementation of the Command Pattern. It maintains a stack of executed commands, permitting multiple levels of undo operations.

```cpp
class CommandManager {
public:
    void execute(Command* cmd){
        cmd->execute();
        cmd_stack.push(cmd);
    }
    void undo() {
        if (!cmd_stack.empty()){
            Command* cmd = cmd_stack.top();
            cmd->undo();
            cmd_stack.pop();
        }
    }
private:
    std::stack<Command*> cmd_stack;
};
```

13.2. E-commerce Transaction Management

The e-commerce realm offers another fertile ground for the application of the Command Pattern. The paradigm of 'undoable operations' provides an effective way to manage transactions, taming the inherent complexity of transactional e-commerce systems.

Let's consider a scenario where an e-commerce platform utilizes commands for various operations - order creation, payment processing, and so on. Each command represents an operation that can be undone.

Here, the Command Pattern shines by providing the ability to undo any transaction (provided the business rules permit such an action). This capability is essential in instances where cancellations and refunds are needed.

13.3. Production Equipment Control

The realm of production and manufacturing invokes a set of sophisticated control systems, often commanding intricate machinery operations. Implementation of undoable operations becomes vital in such environments, offering the capacity to revert inadvertent equipment manoeuvres or decisions, thus ensuring safety and efficiency.

A hypothetical ProductionEquipmentControlCommand could encapsulate several complex operations like 'Start', 'Shutdown', 'Pause', or 'Restart'. The 'undo' method here could reverse any of these commands to the previous state immediately, preventing potential disasters in manufacturing processes.

13.4. Final Remarks

Through these pragmatic examples, we can discern the immensely adaptable nature of the Command Pattern. The offered correlations underline how its use in implementing undoable operations can streamline complex routines, offer safety nets and enhance overall performance in various software systems.

While the adaptiveness of the pattern is itself impressive, the simplicity it introduces in comparison to potentially cumbersome alternative solutions is truly noteworthy. The Command Pattern embodies the adage that powerful solutions can also be elegantly straightforward.

Understanding undoable operations and how to implement them

using the Command Pattern is an essential skill for software developers. Throughout your journey, this knowledge will undoubtedly unravel an easier path through the complexities of software design, empowering you to create more robust and adaptable applications.

Chapter 14. Predicting the Future: The Evolution of the Command Pattern

The story of the Command Pattern is one crammed with continuous evolution. Fascinatingly, even as the software terrain has shifted dramatically over the years, the Command Pattern has held its ground, proving time and again its versatility and indispensable role in building robust applications. In this exploration, we'll attempt to retrospect the myriad ways in which it has metamorphosed, while also forecasting how it might evolve in the coming years.

14.1. DAWN OF THE COMMAND PATTERN

The Command Pattern, one among the GO4's heralded 23 structural designs, was born out of the need for encapsulating an action as an object. It all started with the simple idea of an object representing a request. The command object would house the necessary details, like the method to be executed, its related object, and any parameters required. Early adopters of this pattern lauded its ability to isolate the object that invokes the operation from the one that knows how to execute it.

Though inherently straightforward in its primary form, innovative usage of the Command Pattern by contemporary developers has forged it into a key design technique across a wide array of software applications.

14.2. RESOLVING TEMPORAL COUPLING

As a design pattern, Command facilitates the required separation between the sender and the receiver. The temporal coupling of 'when' an action, such as saving a file, should be performed became decoupled from 'how' it was executed.

This decoupling, combined with the notion of encapsulating requests as objects, proved to be a powerful combination. It allowed developers to schedule operations, create queues of commands to be executed in sequential or specific order, or even to delay execution altogether, thereby introducing more dynamism and flexibility to application fortitude.

14.3. CMD + Z: ENABLING 'UNDO'

One of the most influential modifications in the journey of the Command Pattern has been the introduction of undoable operations. In an increasingly user-centric world, this allowed software applications the graceful ability to rollback to a previous state, often resulting in a substantial boost in user satisfaction and enhanced user experience.

With the Command Pattern at heart, the 'undo' function was implemented by maintaining a history stack of executed command objects, engaging a mechanism to revert to a previous application state when necessary. In this way, a design pattern initially erected for decoupling achieved newfound relevance in boosting application usability.

14.4. THE MACRO COMMAND: A LEAP TOWARDS COMPLEXITY

The incorporation of Macro Command—an advanced derivative of the core Command Pattern—opened a new dimension of complexity. The Macro Command, formed by compiling multiple commands into one, made it possible to execute complex tasks collectively and sequentially via a single invoker.

This improvement, though complex, encouraged developers to manage series of commands in more organized and efficient ways. The impact on reducing code redundancy and enhancing code modularity was remarkable, undoubtedly contributing to the popularity and longevity of the Command Pattern.

14.5. COMMAND + DECORATOR: AN EXHIBITION OF COMPOSABILITY

Composability sprung up as a major feature in evolving design patterns, with various patterns interlocking to form more effective solutions. As an example, the Decorator pattern, used alongside the Command Pattern, simulates the Layer Supertype design pattern. This composite design unleashes the pattern's potential by stringing commands together, thus offering more sophisticated command sequencing.

14.6. TOWARDS AN EVENT-DRIVEN FUTURE

The fast-paced, event-driven nature of the modern web has resulted in an increased demand for designs which manage high-velocity, asynchronous, and distributed data. The Command Pattern's inherent strengths align perfectly with these needs. It shines in situations such as managing events in an event-driven architecture, handling transactions in a distributed system, or ushering successful implementation of the CQRS (Command Query Responsibility Segregation) pattern.

For future iterations, we can hypothesize a stronger foothold for the Command Pattern in both small and large scale applications. It could be adapted to a broader range of scenarios in order to facilitate more efficient, modular, and robust software design. While we cannot predict the exact form it will take, it is apparent from the pattern's history that continuous adaptation and transformation are well-rooted within its core.

Even as the discourse around design patterns evolves towards concurrent programming, microservices, serverless architectures, and more, the Command Pattern's time-tested principles retain their relevance. Rooted in simple yet elegant ideology, the Command Pattern's journey from a humble encapsulator to an enabler of advanced system controllability is evidence of its adaptability—a trait that promises its vigor in the future of software design. As the dynamism of software development continues to stride forward, the Command Pattern will undoubtedly play a seminal role in shaping its evolution.

Chapter 15. Bringing It All Together: Best Practices for Implementing Undoable Operations

Designing and implementing the undoable operations in an application presents a unique challenge, but when executed properly, it can significantly improve the user's experience and boost the overall quality of your software. Herein, we will elaborate on the best practices to ensure the effective implementation of this powerful feature.

15.1. Thou Shalt Know Thine Command

For undoable operations, the command object must encapsulate not just the action, but also the state necessary to undo the action later, if required. This containment of pre-action and post-action state in an object promotes the separation of concerns, as each command object just has to know how to reverse its own action. For instance, a 'setText' command on a text field would store both the old text and new text. Offering an 'undo' method would mean returning the text field to its old content.

```
class SetTextCommand implements Command {
  private String oldText;
  private String newText;
  private TextField field;

  SetTextCommand(TextField field, String newText) {
```

```java
      this.oldText = field.getText();
      this.newText = newText;
      this.field = field;
    }

    @Override
    public void execute() {
      field.setText(newText);
    }

    @Override
    public void undo() {
      field.setText(oldText);
    }
  }
```

15.2. Defining a Command Stack

To provide a sequence of undoable operations, maintain all command objects within an ordered stack-like structure. This command stack follows the LIFO (Last-In-First-Out) principle, where the most recently executed command is the first one to be undone.

```java
class CommandStack {
  private Deque<Command> commandStack; // LIFO Data
Structure

  CommandStack() {
    commandStack = new ArrayDeque<>();
  }

  void executeCommand(Command command) {
    command.execute();
    commandStack.push(command);
```

```java
    }

  void undoLastCommand() {
    if(!commandStack.isEmpty()){
      Command lastCommand = commandStack.pop();
      lastCommand.undo();
    }
  }
}
```

Remember, an undoable operation does not exist in isolation. Rather, it's part of an interlaced network of commands that contribute to the overall functionality of your application.

15.3. Implementing the Redo Operation

The Redo operation is nearly as crucial as Undo, bringing a command back to life after it's been undone. This can be implemented by maintaining a stack of undone commands. When an operation is undone, it's moved from the executed command stack to the undone command stack, and when it's redone, it's moved back to executed stack.

```java
class CommandStack {
  private Deque<Command> commandStack; // For executed
commands
  private Deque<Command> undoneStack;  // For undone
commands

  CommandStack() {
    commandStack = new ArrayDeque<>();
    undoneStack = new ArrayDeque<>();
  }
```

```
    // Other methods omitted for brevity...

    void redoLastCommand() {
      if(!undoneStack.isEmpty()) {
        Command lastUndoneCommand = undoneStack.pop();
        lastUndoneCommand.execute();
        commandStack.push(lastUndoneCommand);
      }
    }

    void undoLastCommand() {
      if(!commandStack.isEmpty()) {
        Command lastCommand = commandStack.pop();
        lastCommand.undo();
        undoneStack.push(lastCommand);
      }
    }
}
```

Note: nullifying or clearing the undoneStack is necessary when a new command is executed after some commands have been undone. This prevents inconsistencies.

15.4. Beyond Undo-Redo – Designing the Command History

Building an undo-redo operation is just the tip of the iceberg. The same principle can be applied to create an elaborate command history. Usually found in high-end software, this feature provides an interactive list of performed actions, allowing users to jump to a specific state in the history.

Building a command history involves maintaining a list of executed command objects in your command stack swap with an appropriate data structure. This grants linear access to the stack, enabling jumps to particular commands or actions.

```
class CommandHistory {
  private List<Command> commandHistory; // For executed
commands

  CommandHistory() {
    commandHistory = new ArrayList<>();
  }

  void executeCommand(Command command) {
    command.execute();
    commandHistory.add(command);
    // Clear everything after the command we've just
executed.

commandHistory.subList(commandHistory.indexOf(command)+1
, commandHistory.size()).clear();
  }

  void jumpToCommand(Command commandInHistory) {
    int indexOfCommand =
commandHistory.indexOf(commandInHistory);
    for(int i=commandHistory.size()-1;
i>=indexOfCommand;i--){
      commandHistory.get(i).undo();
    }
  }
}
```

This added complexity does increase the required resources, but the benefit it provides often outweighs the cost, especially for more advanced applications.

In conclusion, the Command Pattern when wedded to undoable operations, renders a sophisticated tool that can significantly elevate the user experience, accommodate complex interactions, and offer a granular level of control over an application's operations. Remember to consider how each piece interacts in the grander picture, and you'll be well-equipped to implement these useful functionalities.